Egypt
# Classical Art Tours

# Karnak and Luxor

Alessandro Roccati

Translated by Eurolingua, Professional Language Services Ltd,
15-16 Newman Street, Oxford Street, London W1P 3HD

Original title: Karnak e Luxor

Chief editors of ,,Classical Art Tours":
Silvio Locatelli und Marcello Boroli

© Manfred Pawlak Verlagsgesellschaft mbH, Herrsching
Distributed in the UK by Hawk Books Ltd

© Instituto Geografico de Agostini SpA, Novara

# The House of Amun, King of the Gods

One of the most important religious and political centres of the Egypt of the Pharaohs was developed during the second millennium BC on the right bank of the Nile, 750 kilometres from Cairo, in the fertile plain which opens into a broad bed along which the river flows in an east-west direction. Its ruins still survive today. Its history began in a centre of civilisation near the area we know today as Karnak and rapidly expanded to include the present provincial capital of Luxor. It was spurred on by the princes of the region of Thebes who, during the XI Dynasty, conquered Egypt and provided a new race of pharaohs. Although Thebes was only periodically the capital, and the seat of government was once more moved to the north during the XII Dynasty and again during the second half of the XVIII Dynasty, its spiritual supremacy had left its mark on every other Egyptian city.

After expelling the Hyksos, the pharaohs of the New Kingdom (XVIII-XX Dynasties) dedicated themselves single-mindedly to conquest, extending Egypt's protectorate to Palestine, Syria and Nubia. They brought back vast numbers of war trophies which were mainly used to glorify the great sanctuary of Amun. The opulence of its decoration can be seen in the paintings and inscriptions on the surviving walls. One of these relates how, at the end of the thirteenth century BC, Merenptah erected "a great gateway to Amun-Re, its surface covered with gold, with the god's ram-like head encrusted with real lapis lazuli and covered in gold and many precious stones – like nothing ever made before – with a threshold adorned with silver". Now only ruins remain.

Precious materials, especially gold, silver and lapis lazuli could be seen everywhere inside the temple. In places they were replaced with the appropriate colour paint, used with complete symbolic meaning: gold, for example, was thought to originate from the sun.

However, it is the stone, the most important part which has lasted to the present day, reinforcing the belief in its eternal life. The extensive use of a variety of stone differing in durability and composition – limestone, sandstone, quartzite, granite, basanite – both in the construction of walls and for monuments like statues and obelisks, made the ancient Egyptian temples into an appropriately impressive alternative to the building of burial grounds. In any case, although only the walls are still standing, they are almost always covered with reliefs and inscriptions which do not refer to the world of the dead in any way. They reflect the importance which the ancient Egyptians placed on religion and, in a temple like the one at Karnak, contain very important references to historical events in the country's history. Knowledge of the Theban temples, those of Karnak and Luxor being the greatest, therefore provides incredible scope for "reconstructing" the Egyptian civilisation of a whole epoch – the New Kingdom (1570–1070 BC) – in line with large amounts of information retrieved from the Valley of the Kings, on the opposite bank of the Nile.

In ancient times, the great Temple of Amun, the heart of the sacred area of Karnak, was entered via one of two approaches: by river (from the west) or by land (from the south). From either side, the entrance to the temple was heralded by a row of imposing pylons, structures resembling two great towers enclosing a portico ("pylon" in Greek), probably deriving from military architecture. These gateways were responsible for Thebes' reputation, echoed in Homer, as "Thebes of the hundred gates". The pylons are also without doubt the origin of Karnak's name, since in Arabic it means fortification.

The main approach from the Nile was straightforward and led to the cella. However, those who made their approach from Luxor, through the long avenue of sphinxes with their human heads, entered through the southern propylaeum leading to the enclosed courtyard between the third and fourth pylons. From here, one entered the temple itself. It was called *Ipet-sut*, "the most noble seat". Altogether there were three pylons to the west (numbered 1–3) and four from the south (numbered 10–7) leading into the sanctuary which was preceded by three more (numbered 4–6).

A trip around the great Temple of Karnak cannot take the same shape as chronological development. In fact this national Egyptian sanctuary was extended in area rather than height. Each time an extension was required, it was constructed in front of the existing entrance, and unwanted structures were eventually removed and used as building material. The traces of a great number of pharaohs remain, if not in the structure at least in the wall decoration, although all other types have been lost. Some of these can be seen today. During an extraordinarily long period lasting until the Roman Empire, many of those who served the god Amun also carried out a great deal of rearranging, rebuilding, structural restoration and new decoration. This, more than its present ruined state, is the

reason why the site is not straightforward and why it sometimes appears to be a complicated labyrinth. Karnak became a monument of Egyptian history, a mass of ruins and vestiges of a distant past, bearing witness to the deeds of kings and priests, the story of their lives often forming the decorative themes on its vast walls.

The rise of the temple of Karnak to becoming the main centre of worship implies that the god venerated here had become a very important deity. The god Amun was very insignificant during the Memphis period when the Heliopolis theology was dominant (with the sun god Re the leading figure). However, after 2000 BC, he gradually became the supreme Being for all those who acknowledged the pharaoh's authority and also took on the name Amunrasonthèr "Amun (identified with) Ra (sun god of Heliopolis), king of the gods". A Phoenician prince told the Egyptian navigator Unamòn that he had come in search of wood for the god's sacred barque: "Amun created all lands. He created them and created the land of Egypt first, from whence I came. It was there that I gained the knowledge to reach this place. It was there that I gained the wisdom to reach this place.".

The cult of Amun was officially consecrated in Karnak and was founded on a strict theology. It was far removed from the simple faith of the people but they turned to it with spontaneous devotion, granting sacred honours to the ram and Nile goose, the animals through which the god manifested himself as a living being: "Amun-Re, of great anger and great mercy, (first) you made me mistake day for the night, (then) you lifted the darkness from my eyes and forgave me. Amun-Re, you are the adored one, you are the only one to grant pardon even in anger. . .”

Traces of Amun's origins are lost, obscured by earlier gods with which the cult competed and accepted Amun's fate during this historical period. The traditional god of the Thebes region was the god of war, Montu, and the most ancient Min, god of the adjoining Coptic region, also shared many liturgical functions with Amun in Karnak.

## Extension, Reconstruction and Restoration

The Middle Kingdom sanctuary (2000–1700 BC), which was located in the centre of the whole complex, is no longer visible, since its fine limestone walls were used for lime. Some architectural evidence has been recently found in the rear walls, including a beautiful Sesostris I shrine (1971–1928 BC).

During the New Kingdom, Thebes became "the city of Amun" (the Bible's Noamun, called Diospolis by the Greeks). It was compared to Heliopolis, where the first great religion of the united Egypt originated. At this stage, the Karnak complex contained at least three great, sacred areas each of which was made up of temples and secular buildings surrounded by a wall. Amun's enclosure was at the centre, totally isolated with its perimeter of over two kilometres. To the north of it stood the enclosure dedicated to the local god, Montu and, to the south, that of the goddess Mut, Amun's partner god or companion. Archaeological excavation which still continues today, has brought to light other buildings outside these enclosures, for a great number of other gods gradually became part of Amun's family and entourage. Even Osiris,

god of the dead, had many chapels and an official cult within the same principal sanctuary.

After the decline of the Middle Kingdom, a foreign people, the Hyksos, began to rule over Egypt. At the end of a great war of liberation, the pharaohs of the new born New Kingdom tried to return to the flourishing years of the XII Dynasty. The religious reorganisation undoubtedly began in the sanctuary of Amun where the first buildings to change were those of the Middle Kingdom. Around them were built various chapels for statues of the builder/pharaoh and his predecessors, who in this way became associated with the divine cult. Between the fourteenth and fifteenth centuries BC, two rows of chapels were put up all the way round, the first by Amenophis I, later rebuilt by Tuthmosis III, and the second by Queen Hatshepsut.

The sanctuary had already contained a building annex at the rear, converted by Tuthmosis III into an elegant columned hall named after "Tuthmosis III reigning supreme amongst his monuments" and normally referred to as the Festival hall. At first this was used for celebrations of the king's resurrection: after his death, he was absorbed into Osiris and joined the sun, Re. We are told that in the late Pharaonic age the mysteries of Osiris were celebrated on this site, as they were annually in all the main Egyptian temples.

The importance gained by the Amun cult during the New Kingdom was a contributing factor to the distortion of the sanctuary's original purpose. Nevertheless, it maintained all the characteristics of an Egyptian temple, and remained in some ways, a "palace" of Amun. There was a cella for a statue of the god in the innermost section. In front of this was a room for offerings which were placed on specially built shelves. Access to this private area was reserved for the pharaoh or, in his absence, his high priest. Before it stood the so-called Festival Courtyard which was open to audiences of the general public for trials and ceremonies. These areas were altered and decorated but their basic function was not changed.

The first pylons (the fourth. fifth and sixth) were probably built in the reign of Tuthmosis I, in place of the previous brick structures, although they were decorated later. Between the reigns of the great pharaohs Amenophis III (1386–1349 BC) and Ramses II (1279–1212 BC), two very tall pylons were completed, enclosing the Hypostyle Hall. The first pylon was a first millennium invention, but too big to be completed. Various structures were included behind this and were at first built in an empty space: a small Temple of Seti II (1199–1193 BC) built "to revere, honour and implore" the Theban Triad (Amun, Mut and Khons), and a more complex building consecrated by Ramses III (1182–1151 BC). These had already been part of the temple of Sesonchis I (945–924 BC), founder of the XXII Dynasty (called "Bubastite" after the city of Bubastis), situated in a courtyard bordered by two porticos and a pylon (the first) had probably been planned as a gateway to it.

In this courtyard, in front of the first pylon, the pharaoh of the XXIV "Ethiopian" Dynasty, Taharqa (690–644 BC), erected one of the majestic "kiosk" entrances. It was almost a copy of that of Amenophis III and all that remains is one very tall column which would originally have had a lateral wooden covering.

Thanks to modern restoration work and reinforcement of the ruins, the visitor is immediately impressed by the architecture. This work has also uncovered a large amount of objects, lost during rebuilding and demolition, which the pylons and foundations contained like huge favissae. Fires and looting were frequent occurrences: firstly in the period of Assurbanipal in 656 BC, and again during the uprising of 85 BC. During the last century, the tenth pylon was destroyed by dynamite. Although their foundations were poor, the monuments have survived other natural disasters caused by seeping water, floods (one was recorded during the time of Taharqa) and earthquakes, the most memorable of which was in 27 BC.

However, the main and most serious threat to the sanctuary occurred at the height of its splendour. In the temple at Karnak, it is probable that religious thinking before the introduction of a monotheist cult was developing towards a transcendent deity in the form of the solar disc Atum. The application of this theory can be seen during the enlightened reign of Amenophis III but it was his successor, Amenophis IV, known as Akhenaten "prophet of Aton", who carried out the radical reform of the cult. With his religious politics, this pharaoh struck the hardest blow to the development of traditional worship and even banished the name of Amun, so that it was erased from all monuments. A new capital was founded at El Amârna dedicated to the worship of the only universal god, Aton to whom a sanctuary was erected to the east of Amun's enclosure in Karnak. When this "heresy" had ended, thousands of the stone blocks in the walls of the Temple of Atum, decorated with brightly coloured scenes known by their Arabic name *talatàt*), were reused for the Hypostyle Hall and the insides of the later pylons.

The Temple of Karnak's return to the traditional cult of the god Amun is reported on the *restoration stele*, today located in the Egyptian Museum in Cairo, which shows an edict by Tutankhamen (1334–1325 BC). This stele was placed at the north-east corner of the future Hypostyle Hall and a copy was also placed in Montu's enclosure. After the reconsecration of the temple at the end of the El Amârna schism, elaborate reliefs were added. The trend towards the "colossal", favoured from the beginning of the XVIII Dynasty, particularly by Amenophis III, meant that some of the most daring buildings were built by Tutankhamen's successors – Haremhab, Seti I (1291–1279 BC) and Ramses II.

Temple architecture was adorned with objects which were important for the purposes of the cult, but bore no particular relationship to the structure of its walls. The erection of pairs of obelisks had obvious solar symbolism, these being amongst the boldest granite monoliths. They usually stood in front of the temple entrances. That of Tuthmosis I is the only one remaining today of an entire group once standing in front of the fourth pylon. The gigantic obelisks put up in only seven months by Queen Hatshepsut between the fourth and fifth pylons – the obelisk still standing today measures 29.5m – provided the subject for an entire wall of decorative reliefs in this queen's funeral temple at Deir el-Bahri. Nevertheless, these obelisks were walled in to hide them from the sight of her nephew and rival Tuthmosis III. He then erected another pair of obelisks in front of the fourth pylon. This pharaoh can also boast responsibility for the largest obelisk ever – over 33m – although, because of its proportions, it was not built until the reign of Tuthmosis IV. Unlike the others, this was a single obelisk and was placed in the small Temple of Amun Answerer of Prayers, situated behind the large temple for visitors excluded from the main temples. Ramses II enlarged this temple and Taharqa built one of his kiosks in front of it, facing east. In 357 AD, Emperor Constantine II arranged for this obelisk to be taken to the Great Arena in Rome, and since 1587 it has been situated near the Church of St John Lateran. References to its removal can still be found on the ruined walls along the path to the Nile. Many of the obelisks were demolished but two made from electrum, 7m tall and once located in front of the sixth pylon, were removed by the Assyrians in 656 BC.

One feels the protective presence of the gods in the many majestic avenues of sphinxes which, whether forming approaches to the temples or links between the sanctuaries, were an original feature of the buildings in the Thebes area. Some of the sphinxes resemble rams, the sacred animal of Amun, while some have a pharaoh's head, in keeping with solar symbolism. The oldest probably date back to Amenophis III. The avenue joining Karnak to the Temple of Luxor dates from Nectanebo I (378–360 BC). Other statues, with a human figure attached to a lion's head, were carved in the hundreds during the reign of Amenophis III and placed around some of the sanctuaries as protection. The goddess Sekhmet is one of these.

The walls of Karnak themselves bear countless drawings and inscriptions which can give a far better account of community life in Egypt than literature or history. Enormous statues were dedicated by the pharaohs. The colossus of Amenophis III, the base of which survives in front of the tenth pylon, was comparable in its original dimensions (18m in height) to the so-called Memnon colossus which stood in front of this sovereign's funeral temple and which can still be seen today on the opposite bank of the Nile. The statue of Ramses II, considered a masterpiece of Egyptian sculpture, is in Turin. It was discovered lying in pieces with others in the temple dedicated to Ptah.

There were very many smaller statuettes of priests and dignitaries filling every possible space and representing an entire stratum of privileged society. Many of these were eventually removed and buried in a deep pit near the seventh pylon, in the courtyard which takes its name from this "hiding place". This favissa dates back to the end of the Ptolemaic period and has preserved a real treasure trove of antiquities. As well as architectural remains, 751 statues and 17,000 bronzes were found at a depth of fourteen metres. Numerous steles, also dedicated to private citizens, were used even in ancient times as building material or palimpsests.

## Historical Findings

The pharaohs' presence dominated the large reliefs which cover the external walls of the main sanctuary and were, therefore, visible to everybody. On the north side of the Hypostyle Hall, are the fine illustrations of battle scenes and campaigns against the Asians and Libyans, first commissioned by Seti I. His successor, Ramses II, followed suite and had many versions of the *Poem of Kadesh* made, dedicating them to the epic battle which he fought against the Hittites, so making a mon ment out of this literary work. Ramses II's depicted surrounded by enemy ranks, his ca for help to the god Amun on the battlefield m raculouly echoing through the forest of c lumns in the Hypostyle Hall, so that the g hears him and goes to his rescue:

*Here I pray on the borders of a foreign land,*
*and my voice echoes in southern Heliopolis [Karnak*
*I discovered that Amun had heard my call:*
*he gave me his hand and I took courage.*

The poem was reproduced twice on th Hypostyle Hall's southern external wal firstly, on the walls of the "hiding place courtyard, where the hieroglyphic text of th treaty between Egyptians and Hittites is als inscribed; and again on the external wa which closes the western side of the souther propylaum. A further copy decorates th façade of the pylon in the Temple of Luxor.

The friendship between Egypt and th Hittites, a warlike Indo-European people wh had established a powerful kingdom in Asi Minor, was also celebrated officially with th large, commemorative inscriptions describin Ramses II's two later marriages to Anatolia princesses. A copy was "posted" on the south ern façade of the ninth pylon (east tower), th one differing from another long text know as "Ptah's blessing" (on the west tower). An other copy, incised on one large block of al baster, can be found in Mut's enclosure.

Pharaoh Merenptah (1212–1202 BC) ha the inside of the "hiding place" courtyard de corated with scenes of his victories ove Libya. However, this eastern wall was par tially demolished to create a passage-wa when Tuthmosis III's obelisk (now in front c the Lateran Church) was removed. A copy o the so-called "Israel stele" was also situate near the seventh pylon. In biblical style it commemorated the pharaoh's conquests in the Land of Canaan, and the name of Israel was mentioned for the very first time.

The custom of laying out a written report of important military and political events inside the sanctuary was not just for propaganda, but also to ensure divine protection. This is also evident, though less obviously so, in Pharaoh Tuthmosis III's dedication of an entire chamber in front of the sixth pylon, to reproducing war diaries describing the difficult conquest of Palestine and Syria (Hall of Annals). Two electrum obelisks stood inside the hall, and two granite pillars with the heraldic plants of the Delta and the Valley of the Nile can still be found there today. Tuthmosis III wanted the account of the ceremony of the oracle, by which he was called to the throne, to be nearby. Long lists of victories, overthrown cities and subjugated peoples in Nubia and Asia decorated both the entrance to the Hall of Annals and the side of the south propylaeum.

At the very beginning of the New Kingdom, Pharaoh Kamose (who died about 1570 BC) put up a double stele (found recently) relating the banishment of the Hyksos. The custom of writing the official version of certain events on stone tablets was later continued by many pharaohs who dedicated copies to the main temples. During the XXII Dynasty, Prince Osorkon had a wall, erected to connect the second pylon to the Temple of Ramses III (The Gateway of the Bubastites), decorated with a "chronicle" which has become a valuable source of information about a little-known period. Sesonchis I also had inscribed lists of cities conquered during his campaigns in Palestine against the Judaic kingdoms and Israel.

## Cult Rituals

More religious scenes were kept for the internal walls, particularly in the Hypostyle Hall where there was a full report of daily cult rituals.

Papyrus examples of holy books used for the Karnak cult of the XXII Dynasty (Bubastite period, circa ninth century BC) are kept in Berlin. The entire sanctuary library was lost in fires and looting, but it is probable that some traces of it survived and copies, found on the opposite bank of the Nile in the Theban burial grounds, used for liturgical ceremonies there.

The rituals consisted of a long series of prayers and acts carried out around the statue of the god at various times during the day fitting in with morning investiture as well as eating certain foods and other ceremonies intended to attract the gods' favour. No doubt a great number of priests had a special rôle in the ceremony and were obliged to perform certain ritual duties such as washing in the sacred lake four times a day. The most important aspects of the rituals were enacted during the celebrations of frequent and impressive festivals (fifty-four a year had been registered during the reign of Tuthmosis III), when the divine statue was carried along in a procession, on a sacred barque. The priests, ranked in order of seniority, often wore special ancient costumes. The processions gathered in the courtyard between the ninth and tenth pylons where numerous steles and statues had been placed. Oracles were also present and there was a form of public worship.

The great festival of Opet (Luxor), in which Amun departed from his sanctuary, is the decorative theme for the external walls of the temple erected by Ramses III as well as for the Temple of Luxor.

The god, who was asked questions during the procession, gave oracular replies. In fact, one of the temples' prerogatives was intervention in the country's affairs: from the most trivial administering of justice to the appointment of priests and approving the eventual choice of the pharaoh, the temple's greatest privilege. Divine manifestation took the form of certain movements in the effigy of the god during the procession. One of the Tuthmosis III texts relates how, while Amun's statue was being moved into the festival courtyard, the sudden increase in its weight caused the priests carrying the effigy to turn in the direction of the future sovereign, designating him as the successor to the throne. Reliable proof of these decisions was kept and one example, dated 651 BC, has been discovered signed by more than fifty witnesses.

There were various ways in which officials were called to the highest office of "first priest of Amun". Some, like Bakenkhonsu who was summoned to the temple of Ramses II at the end of a career in which he gradually rose to the highest rank, had lived completely within the sanctuary walls. Some were appointed by other sanctuaries, like Nebunenef from Abydos but this was always subject to the pharaoh's approval or intervention. However, at the end of the New Kingdom the position became hereditary, which resulted in, as it were, dynasties of armed priests who defended their own cities. In 850 BC, Osorkon II granted political autonomy to Thebes. The combination of religious, cultural, political and economic interests focusing on the sanctuary of Amun gave the temple exceptional prestige and meant extraordianry privi-

leges for its hierarchy of priests who elevated the religious office of high priest to the status of the pharaoh. An entire population of cult worshippers, from theologians to artists, gravitated round this eminent figure, as well as hundreds of different kinds of servants, while brides were quite often employed as chanters of the gods, too. Dwellings of high-ranking priests, living in various times from Sesostris I to the Ptolemaic period, have been found on the banks of the sacred lake. Many of their graves, sometimes as elaborate as mausoleums, have been found on the opposite bank of the Nile.

Inventories of possessions, festival calendars and lists of gifts were inscribed on the temple walls like monuments guaranteeing perpetual faithful observance. The Temple of Karnak was the richest economic centre in ancient Egypt and continually benefited from royal allowances. The Harris papyrus, the longest one known (40m), kept in the British Museum in London, lists an incredible number of donations given by Ramses III alone. Its authenticity was proved by slightly more recent lists. Next to the places of worship were found a large number of store-rooms, "treasuries" for precious objects, depositories for incense or food, workshops for making materials for cult worship, as used for Shabaka's "place of gold" (716–702 BC) on the northern side of the Hypostyle Hall, enclosures for breeding birds (near the lake), gardens and so forth.

Two rooms with particularly outstanding reliefs are located near Tuthmosis III's Festival Hall. One of the reliefs reproduces exotic plants and animals collected by this pharaoh during his military campaigns, (hence its name "botanical garden") and provides a figurative complement to the inscriptions of the *Annals*. Another room, called the Chapel of Ancestors, was for ritual offerings made to all the earlier kings, represented by statues in the sanctuary. These reliefs are now in the Louvre.

During the obscure period following the New Kingdom, when Egypt had declined into feudal anarchy, the tendency to both build and maintain existing buildings had diminished. Makeshift houses were put up next to the sacred buildings and it was the High Priest Menkheperra who decided "to erect a very large wall to the north of Karnak... to hide the temple and its father, Amun-Re, and clear it of the people, having found it cluttered with Egyptian dwellings in Amun's enclosure. The base [of the wall] – which he totally rebuilt – was a wall built [with a facing] of basanite. The people of Thebes were expelled from the enclosure of their father, Amun-Re, to sanctify the abode of the sacred one in his abode".

The task of restoring past respectability fell to Taharqa, a pharaoh from Nubia. Keeping to his country's beliefs, he carried out intensive building projects and readjusted the accepted theological structure of the cult: "It is thee Amun, it is thee Shu, thou art the highest of all gods, thou art he who sublimely manifests himself like the four winds of the sky..." A small theological *summa* was discovered in one of the Taharqa buildings, in the ruined building near the sacred lake.

Another Nubian pharaoh, Piankhy (747–716 BC) tried to resolve the political problem of the excessive independence of the Amun priesthood by attributing greater importance to the pharaohs' queens, equally represented in his religion. From the XXI Dynasty, the king's daughters were "divine worshippers of Amun" and assisted the high priest in running the temple. The divine consort Amenardis, of Nubian lineage, was selected by means of adoption as heiress to the existing consort Shepenwepet I, a process which continued. Chapels erected by these important figures, from that late period, can be seen between the Hypostyle Hall and the Temple of Ptah, and in the Montu enclosure. Two important epigraphs, known as the "adoption steles" (of Nitocris, daughter of Psammetichus I and by Shepenwepet II, daughter of Piankhy) and the "endowment steles" from the XXIII Dynasty (Amun's decree to sanction a gift of land) were found on the façade of the Temple of Seti II in the first courtyard.

## Other Temples

The great sanctuary of Amun has left behind the most impressive ruins. However, even though the structures of the nearby enclosures dedicated to the god Montu and goddess Mut have been razed to the ground, there are still traces of the huge building programme begun by Amenophis III, also responsible for the temple of Luxor. Of similar size, the temples of Montu and Mut, in their respective enclosures, were probably extensions of older buildings. The architecture was later adjusted at various stages.

Montu was the god of war, originating from the Thebes region and worshipped in the form of a bull. One of his main sanctuaries, dating from the Middle Kingdom, is situated slightly to the north of Karnak, at Medamud, the Greek Keramiké. A small temple dedicated to the goddess Maat, patron of universal order, was located in the Montu enclosure where, during the reign of Ramses XI (1098–1070 BC), an investigation into tomb robberies was carried out.

Mut was the companion goddess of Amun and his enclosure still contains numerous statues of the goddess Sekhmet who was associated with her. Hundreds of these were made in Amenophis III's workshops. The small oval lake of which Mut was mistress can still be seen behind the enclosure. Although the remaining ruins are scanty, even including the main sanctuary of Mut and a minor temple erected by Ramses III in her honour, they are very evocative. There can be no doubt that the original importance and splendour of the decoration equalled those in Amun's sanctuary, and that the development of Mut's enclosure ran parallel with it. This enclosure was entered from the north on the same axis as the southern propylaeum of the Temple of Amun, to which it was connected by an avenue of sphinxes with rams' heads (criosphinxes). It seems that it was also dedicated by Amenophis III although other sovereigns later replaced his name with their own (Haremhab, Seti II, Herihor).

The Theban Triad of gods had their own sanctuary. Although older reliefs suggest that something existed before, the sanctuary was built by Ramses III and some of his successors and is still well preserved. The High Priest Herihor (circa 1075 BC) and his immediate successor Pinodem I, representing themselves as pharaohs, decorated the first courtyard with their own names. In front of the pylon, Taharqa added a "kiosk" with tall columns, later razed to the ground. During the Byzantine period, a church built inside the temple was consecrated.

The Temple of Khons, the third god of the Triad, is situated half way between the Temple of Amun and the Temple of Mut, next to the southern propylaeum. It was probably not enclosed within the walls of the Amun complex until the time of Nectanebo I. The walls were originally about 25m tall and their great gateways were the pride of the Ptolemaic Dynasty which followed, and particularly of the great sovereign Ptolemy III Euergetes I (246–222 BC).

On the roof of the Temple of Khons was an important astronomical observatory, used for establishing the calendar and the times for celebrations and festivals. Because Khons was a moon god, statues of sacred moon baboons were placed in the courtyard. We have no specific information about another important rôle of the temple: healing the sick, but the fact that the god Khons was worshipped publicly shows his importance as a healing god. A report written during the Ptolemaic period and transcribed onto a stele, today kept in Paris but discovered not far from this temple, tells how the statue of the god had been taken as far as Bactria to heal a princess possessed by evil spirits.

The minor temple dedicated to the goddess Opet is situated next to the Temple of Khons. Because this goddess was likened to Isis, the building was also the seat of the Osiris cult. This temple was put up by Tuthmosis III during the XVIII Dynasty and was renewed by Taharqa almost a thousand years later. Various sacella in honour of Osiris were located in the eastern part of the Amun enclosure and dedicated to different aspects of the god.

Tuthmosis III also erected the stone temple of Ptah, situated at the outer edge of the area dedicated to Montu. He had found a crumbling, bare brick building which must have been the original condition of most of the structures before their restoration as monuments.

## The Temple of Luxor

This was certainly the main satellite of the great centre of Karnak to which it was linked by both the cult and the shared history which shaped its architecture and decorative features. Luxor and Karnak were also directly connected to the Temple of Nectanebo I and to each other via the majestic, three kilometre long avenue of sphinxes with human heads.

Some monuments certainly existed in Luxor from the time of the Middle Kingdom, as is borne out by the way the topography corresponds with the temples on the opposite bank of the Nile and by the re-use of older materials in the temple such as an architrave of Sebekhotep II, pharaoh of the XIII Dynasty. Nevertheless, the architectural development of the site began with the building, with its impressive colonnades, put up by Amenophis III, the great pharaoh who first made Thebes famous all over the world. The architect who created the temple was probably Amenophis, son of Hapu, renowned for his knowledge and later venerated as a god.

The Temple of Luxor was constructed in a north-south direction, parallel both to the bank of the Nile and to the great sanctuary of Karnak, to which it was then connected by a long avenue of sphinxes. The history of the Temple of Luxor ist not as disjointed as that of the great sanctuary of Karnak. Ramses II was the other pharaoh whose name was linked to Luxor. Two centuries after Amenophis III, he emulated him:

*Was it not for you [Amun] that I created so many monuments/that I filled your temple with my trophies?/Was it not for you that I constructed my ancient temple,/and granted everything to you?/I gave you all my land to increase my divine offerings to you,/I offered you tens of thousands of oxen and aromatic herbs,/I omitted nothing in completing your sanctuary,/I erected great stone pylons for you,/I myself raised the pillars./I brought you obelisks from Elephantine,/I myself still bring you blocks of stone...*

These words, from the *Pem of Kadesh*, give the most striking description of Ramses II's buildings in the Temple of Luxor, such as the great pylon which took the place of the two original granite obelisks.

In the Temple of Luxor there are another six impressive statues of Ramses II (two seated and four standing) which are similar to the colossi of various XVIII Dynasty kings in front of the southern propylaea at Karnak. Another extract from the *Poem of Kadesh* is the only decoration on the façade of the two pylon towers, and is a direct testimony to the pharaoh's works.

The courtyard with porticos on three sides opens out behind the pylon. To the right of the entrance, a chapel was built and dedicated to the Theban Triad. A great colonnade erected by Amenophis III leads into a second courtyard in front of a hypostyle hall where, on the left, one sees a very rare copy of the ancient foundation ceremony for temples. All the rituals are described in detail in correct order and the prayers they recited written out. From here we enter the centre of the temple with its chapels dedicated to Mut and Khons and, then, after passing through two vestibules, the room used to contain the sacred barque where Alexander the Macedonian built a fine granite sanctuary similar to that of the Temple of Karnak. Near the rooms used to worship Amun in Luxor, as in the Temple of Karnak, there are also areas dedicated to the pharaoh's godliness, an important theme during this period. The reliefs in one of the east rooms, where the sanctuary was partly demolished, depict the dogma of divine descent, in other words the union between the god Amun and the mother of the queen which gave their pharaoh son superhuman qualities. The scenes dwell upon a description of the meeting between the god and the queen, the birth of Amenophis III, the gods' intervention in his upbringing and the certainty of his good fortune.

During the period of the Roman Empire, the Greco-Roman city of Ophieum (a continuation of the old name Opet) grew up in the Luxor area, becoming the main military centre for all of Upper Egypt and the base of the legions defending the southern borders beyond Aswan. The central room in the middle of the temple, in front of the one containing Alexander's sanctuary, was converted into a Chapel by the legions, so blocking the passage to the inside of the sanctuary. The walls were covered with stuccos and paintings depicting the two Emperors Augustus and the two Caesars, concealing the ancient gods. Niches surmounted by shrines, for the emperors' statues, were carved out of the rear wall. It is here that the public were called to worship. Not far away, a pedestal inscribed with the name of Constantine commemorates the victory of the Christian faith. Coptic churches, ruins of which remain, were later built outside the temple.

Crude brick buildings used for troops' quarters and houses were built beside the long avenues round the temple. A forum was discovered on the eastern side of the temple, and work carried out during Tiberius' time has left numerous commemorative steles. The Arabic name *al-qasr* derives from the Latin *castrum*, and its plural *l-uqsor* was the origin of today's name Luxor.

This summary is very far from being a full description of all the main buildings which, in the distant past, together formed the first great cities of the world, the dwelling places of the gods before man inhabited them.

*Detail of the base of the statue of Ramses II in front of the Temple of Luxor, symbolising the union of Upper and Lower Egypt.*

# The Temple of Karnak

On the preceding pages is an axial view of the Temple of Amun from the entrance, showing the long row of pylons stretching 350 metres. In front of the sanctuary's main entrance is an avenue lined with forty sphinxes with rams' heads, the remains of a longer approach changed over the years, its present layout dating to the Roman period. The pharaohs of the New Kingdom (1570 – 1070 BC) continually enlarged and extended the earlier Temple of Karnak dating back to the Middle Kingdom (2000 – 1700 BC) of which no trace remains. This was probably entered from the site of the present fourth pylon, which was reconstructed in stone together with the fifth and sixth by Tuthmosis I. The pharaoh was succeeded by Queen Hatshepsut who built a chapel for the sacred barque. The chapel was destroyed for political reasons by her nephew Tuthmosis III and replaced by another in granite which, in turn, was rebuilt during the Ptolemaic era by Filippo Arrideo. Tuthmosis III was one of the greatest inspirations behind the Karnak sanctuary and planned, amongst other things, the building complex situated behind the Middle Kingdom sanctuary, and preceded by a long columned hall called the Festival Hall. He was also responsible for the construction of other minor temples nearby, like that of Ptah on the north side of Amun's enclosure, and that of Opet on the south side.

Architectural development then intensified under Amenophis III, the "magnificent" pharaoh. Having demolished a courtyard and peristyle which Tuthmosis IV had erected in front of the fourth pylon, another pylon of impressive dimensions (the third) was built, using building materials from older edifices. A very tall entrance colonnade was built in front of this, preceded by an avenue of sphinxes resembling the layout of the Temple of Luxor and other sanctuaries. In front of this colonnade, Haremhab began the construction of a new pylon (the second) completed by Ramses II. The space in between was filled with the famous Hypostyle Hall. The first pylon was planned by Sesonchis I but was not built until Nectanebo I's reign. However, only two thirds (32m) of this massive structure was completed and it lacks the usual crowning section and decoration.

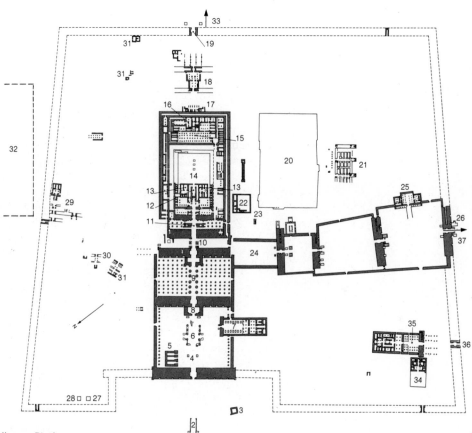

1 Podium or Platform
2 Entrance avenue lined with criosphinxes
3 Chapel of Acoris and Psammuthis
4 First Courtyard
5 Small Temple of Seti II
6 Taharqa Kiosk
7 Temple of Ramses II
8 Bubastite Gateway
9 The Great Hypostyle Hall
10 Tuthmosis I Obelisk
11 Tuthmosis I Hall (re-arranged),
   with Hatshepsut's Obelisk
12 Sanctuary for the Sacred Barque
   reconstructed by Filippo Arrideo
13 Chapels of Hatshepsut
14 Former Site of Middle Kingdom Temple
15 Tuthmosis III's Festival Hall
16 Room called the "Botanical Garden"
17 Tuthmosis III's East Chapel
18 Temple of "Amun Answerer of Prayers",
   where the Lateran obelisk stood
19 Eastern Gateway (Nectanebo I)
20 Sacred Lake (of Amenophis III)
21 XIX-XXIX Dynasty Dwellings and Animal
   Enclosures

22 Taharqa Building in honour of Re-Harakhty,
   next to which is the site of the fallen
   Hatshepsut obelisk
23 Giant Scarabaeus Monument, possibly from
   Amenophis III's Funeral Temple
24 Courtyard of the "Hiding Place" (Favissa)
25 Amenophis II's Festival Hall, reconstructed
   on this site during the reign of Ramses
26 Base of the Amenophis III Colossus,
   completely destroyed
27 White Chapel of Sesostris I, reconstructed
28 Amenophis I's alabaster chapel, reconstructed
29 Temple of Ptah
30 Chapels built by the Divine Consorts
   of Amun
31 Chapels dedicated to Osiris
32 Sacred Enclosure of Montu (the Greeks'
   *Appolloneion*)
33 Approximate location of the Temple of Aton
34 Temple of Opet-Isis (the Greeks' *Demetreion*)
35 Temple of Khons (the Greeks' *Herakleion*)
36 Southern Gateway of Ptolemy III Euergetes II
37 Avenue of Sphinxes with rams' heads leading
   to the Enclosure of Montu (the Greeks' *Hereion*)

*Below: view of the middle cella, dedicated to Amun, of the small temple built by Seti II in the area later included within the temple's first court. Two standing statues of pharaohs stood on each side of the entrance, the larger of which (4.65m tall) is now on display in the Egyptian Museum in Turin. Opposite: the pylon flanked by royal colossi at the entrance of the Temple of Ramses III, built opposite that of Seti II. The peristyle court can be seen with statues of pharaohs portrayed as Osiris.*

The criosphinxes (or sphinxes
with rams' heads) in the first
court (on the left, a detail of the
row) were placed in their
present position in ancient
times when they were removed
from the avenue leading to the
second pylon to make room for
new buildings. This was
probably the "Road of Rams"
referred to in documents of the
time of Ramses. The ram was
identified with Amun even
though the god was usually
represented in human form. A
ram's head was placed at the
bow and stern of his sacred
barque. The criosphinxes also
symbolised the deity who
protected the pharaoh, who is
portrayed between their front
legs. Although others often
claimed them as theirs, these
sphinxes were probably carved
for Amenophis III, the pharaoh
responsible for other avenues of
criosphinxes. One of these
linked the tenth pylon of the
southern propylaea to Mut's
enclosure. Another was in
front of the Temple of Khons,
facing south, then added to the
avenue of sphinxes with
human heads which leads from
the Temple of Luxor. Yet
another avenue of sphinxes
with human heads (the image
of the pharaoh) formed the
entrance to Montu's enclosure
from the north.

*Left: a view of the first court with the remains of columns from the Kiosk of Taharqa. It was a majestic entrance where the processional barque used to pause, and was originally composed of ten columns with open papyrus capitals, 20.70m high and surmounted by a wooden roof. The Ptolemaic decorations of the gateway of the second pylon, erected by Haremhab und Ramses II, and now partly demolished, can be seen behind the columns enclosing the Hypostyle Hall. In the forground one can see a platform used to support the sacred barque.*

*Above: Ramses II carries out the ceremony of incense before Amun's barque, which is carried in procession by priests disguised as mythological creatures. The relief, to be found on the internal wall of the Hypostyle Hall, was originally a bas-relief and later changed with the technique of intaglio. This was much simpler because the figures were carved into the stone instead of the background being cut away around them. The technique was first used only on external walls, but was applied to internal walls at the time of Ramses II.*

*Below: a horse protected by a saddlecloth pulling a chariot on which the pharaoh Tutankhamen is depicted overthrowing his enemies. The block with this relief is a recent discovery found when the second pylon was emptied. It had been used as filling material and this contributed to the preservation of its colours. In Egyptian art, reliefs were always finished by adding pure colours – white, yellow, red, blue and black – used in a conventional way to highlight the symbols (photograph: Roccati).*

*Opposite: view of the colonnade erected by Amenophis III as the temple entrance and later used by Seti I as the central corridor of the Hypostyle Hall (a Greek word meaning hall supported by columns). The central columns, now twelve but probably fourteen originally, are 22.40m high, including the abacus, and 9.90m in circumference. They stand on a wider base, with rounded off corners, and finish with a bell-shaped capital representing the open papyrus flower and contrasting with the other columns in the hall which have a capital representing the closed papyrus bud. In fact, the shapes used in all Egyptian architecture were mainly inspired by nature.*

Seti I was responsible for the reliefs on the external northern wall of the Hypostyle Hall (below) in praise of his military successes. The subjects are divided by the entrance door into the hall: the Asian campaigns in Syria and Canaan on the left wall; the Libyan and Hittite campaigns on the right. Top of this page: Seti I in the traditional position of annihilating his enemies. Opposite: Seti I mounts his chariot behind lines of prisoners. These reliefs mark the beginning of a new form of Egyptian art: the depiction of historical events. Carved on the external walls of the temple, the "deeds of the king" which had previously been handed down through written texts, were now revealed to everyone. On the other hand, religious scenes (portrayals of great festivals, daily celebrations, rituals and so on) depicted on the inside of the sanctuary were accessible to few people and were meant to complete or even to take the place of true worship. In fact, after the priests had "opened their mouths" with the appropriate ritual, the sculpted figures continued to repeat the sacred ceremonies even when they were not actually being performed.

*Opposite: detail of the forest of columns in the Hypostyle Hall erected by Seti I around Amenophis III's central colonnade, between the second and third pylons. This immense hall, the largest in the world with a stone covering, measures 102 by 53m and contains one hundred and twenty columns 14.70m tall divided into nine rows originally of fourteen columns each. Their dimensions, much smaller than the central colonnade, permitted the opening of cloister windows between the architrave and the ceiling (right: photograph by Roccati). Together with the central skylight, they were the main source of light in the hall, which was closed in on all sides by high walls. Both the walls and the columns were later decorated with religious and ritual motifs in honour of Amun and all the gods of Karnak. Every space was filled so that the massive structure of the columns appears to be a sequence of backdrops. The reliefs, begun by Seti I, were completed and partly recarved in the time of Ramses II.*

Eastern view of Amenophis III's middle colonnade in the Hypostyle Hall which can be seen on one side through a breach in the third pylon. This enormous pylon was also Amenophis III's work and he did not hesitate to demolish older, abandoned structures in order to procure his building materials more easily. This attitude towards predecessors' monuments was nothing new in the pharaohs' behaviour, but in Karnak it was particularly common. It was, however, also the reason for the excellent preservation of entire buildings which, buried in this way, were protected from the ravages of time. Sesostris I's so-called White Chapel and a sanctuary for Amenophis I's alabaster barque were recovered from the third pylon and were both reconstructed in Amun's enclosure. Part of the Red Chapel – another sanctuary for Hatshepsut's barque – the remains of an Amenophis II alabaster chapel, a sanctuary for Tuthmosis IV's barque, a Tuthmosis IV peristyle court and statues and steles from as far back as the Middle Kingdom were also recovered.

*Below: the obelisks erected by Tuthmosis I (in the background,*
*by Hatshepsut (in the foreground) in front of the fourth pylor*
*only survivors of the original pairs. Opposite: detail of one of*
*two Hatshepsut obelisks, now lying on the ground. The god A*
*is depicted welcoming the queen. There are remains on the gre*
*of another pair of obelisks put up by Tuthmosis III. The poin*
*tops of these monuments were originally covered in gold leaf*
*reflect the rays of the sun to which the obelisks were dedicated*

Opposite: detail of Tuthmosis III's Hall of Annals, with the two granite pillars decorated with reliefs and the heraldic motifs (lotus and papyrus) of Upper and Lower Egypt. This is a foreshortened picture taken from the adjacent Hypostyle Hall. On this page, a detail of the black granite statue of Tuthmosis III from the Temple of Karnak, kept in the Egyptian Museum in Cairo. It portrays the most famous ancient Egyptian leader, one of the main inspirations behind the sanctuary of Amun in Karnak.

On these two pages are some of the reliefs engraved on blocks of red quartzite found inside the third pylon where they had been used as filling material. They originate from the sanctuary for the sacred barque erected by Queen Hatshepsut where a fourth century BC sanctuary now stands, also meant for the sacred barque and constructed by Filippo Arrideo. Some of the remains of the original Temple of Amun are also visible in this same area. Hatshepsut's structure, commonly known as the Red Chapel, had already been demolished by her successor Tuthmosis III. He replaced it with another, now also in ruins. The reconstruction of this large, important monument is still unfinished but other blocks are in the process of being recovered. The reliefs depict the queen's ritual route during the jubilee festival. She is accompanied by the bull Api and, far right, musicians and dancers perform in honour of Amun. A group of harpists provide musical accompaniment, to two lines of dancers performing various "wheel" acrobatics.

The Festival Hall built by Tuthmosis III, seen from the original site of the god Amun's cella. The hall, 40m long, consists of a rectangular pillared deambulatory enclosing twenty columns of a shape which was totally original for stone architecture. In fact, they were based on the tent-poles used in the jubilee festival "kiosk". On the northern side of the hall there were three chapels perhaps dedicated to the Theban Triad and behind these, a raised chapel with no ceiling dedicated to Re, the sun god.

*Below: a detail of the bas-relief decorating the walls of the room adjacent to the Festival Hall, generally known as the "Botanical Garden". In fact, a great number of different species of animals and plants, brought by Tuthmosis III on his return from the Syrian campaign and offered to the god Amun, are depicted. Opposite: an internal view of the Festival Hall. Some of the columns in this vast area still bear traces of figures painted during the Christian era when the hall was transformed into a church.*

The sacred lake of the Temple of Amun, covering an area equal to one third of the entire sanctuary, was created at the time of Amenophis III. The lake was a common ingredient in sacred Egyptian architecture and was mainly used for ritual washing which the priests had to perform four times a day. The high priests' dwellings were built on the banks and birds were bred for sacred offerings. Various remains of these buildings have been discovered. In the background, the obelisks of Tuthmosis I, in the centre, and Hatshepsut, to the right.

*The huge Scarabaeus monument (opposite), the scarab being an image of the god Kheperi, one of the sun's manifestations, is situated on the banks of the lake. It could have originated from Amenophis III's funeral temple on the opposite bank of the Nile and was placed here by Taharqa to symbolise the solar nature of Amun. Below: a view of the eighth pylon built by Tuthmosis III on the southern side of the temple. The statuesque colossi in front of it, a characteristic of the New Kingdom, portray the pharaoh (photograph: Roccati).*

*Left: Ptolemy III Euergetes I's gateway, opened in the south side of Amun's enclosure in front of the Temple of Khons. He was the third element of the Theban Triad, son of Amun and Mut, worshipped as a moon god and depicted as a boy surrounded by the rising lunar disc. The gateway is decorated with many fine reliefs to which epigraphic copies of important texts have been added. In front of this one can see the bases of the columns from one of the four Taharqa kiosks entering into Amun's sacred enclosure.*

*Above: the Temple of Khons pylon, a fine example of classic Egyptian architecture because of its excellent state of preservation. The top is in particularly good condition. It is crowned with a moulding called the Egyptian Groove, shaped like downwardly concave coving above which there is a flat fascia. The temple was built by XX Dynasty pharaohs, Ramses III in particular, but much of the decoration on the pylon and in the court was the work of the High Priest Herihor.*

*Opposite: the door leading into the cella of the Temple of Khons, behind which there is a quartzite stand used to support the sacred barque on which the divine simulacrum was carried. Deities paying homage to the moon god Khons can be observed on the architrave in the foreground. This part of the sanctuary was built by Ramses III but the decoration of the jambstones was by Ptolemy VIII Euergetes I and dates back to the second century BC. On the western side of the Temple of Khons, stands a building consecrated to the goddess Opet, the divine mother (photograph: Roccati).*

*Above: Sesostris I's White Chapel. It is a fine limestone "kiosk" which contained the sacred barque during the king's jubilee. Its reconstruction is modern (1938) and was made possible by the recovery of all the blocks, used at the time of Amenophis III to fill the cavity inside the third pylon. The monument dates to the oldest period in the temple's history.*

*Opposite: The Ptolemaic propylaea of the Temple of Ptah, comprising six gateways. The temple, on an east-west axis, is located on the north side of Amun's enclosure. It was reconstructed on ancient ruins by Tuthmosis III and dedicated to Ptah, the ancient Egyptian deity considered to be the creator of men and gods. Below: inscription of the emperor Tiberius, engraved on a jambstone of the gateway, mentioning the old sage, Amenophis, son of Hapu, who was probably the architect of Amenophis III's buildings and was honoured like a god (photograph: Roccati).*

*View of Montu's enclosure from the south, with the badly
damaged temple buildings. The main entrance to the Temple of
Montu (god of war and the original lord of the Thebes region) was
to the north, where a gateway built by Ptolemy III Euergetes I was
connected to a platform or embarkation point on the Nile by an
avenue of sphinxes with human heads. In the foreground are the
ruins of a small temple, next to the Temple of Montu, dedicated to
Maat, goddess of truth and cosmic order. The first layout of the
complex dates to the time of Amenophis III.*

The Colossus of Amenophis IV
in the Egyptian Museum,
Cairo. It was found, with the
remains of about thirty others,
during the excavation of a
canal to the east of Amun's
enclosure, on the presumed site
of Aton's. The style of the
statue, closely resembling the
pharaoh, conformed to the new
concept of realist art
encouraged by the radical
sovereign. He introduced to
Karnak the cult of one god –
Aton, the solar disc, – who
replaced all the other gods
including Amun. He built
sanctuaries to Atum, which
were later demolished by his
successors who used many of
these blocks as filling material
for the pylons. Opposite: a
granite statue of the seated
goddess Sekhmet, one of the
artistic creations which
marked the reign of
Amenophis III. Hundreds of
these statues were placed
around some of the temples,
especially in Mut's enclosure, to
the south of Amun's, where this
example is found. Sekhmet
symbolised war and was
depicted with a lion's head.

Shown on these pages is a photograph of the alabaster block on which was inscribed an abbreviated version of the text commemorating Ramses II's marrige to a Hittite princess in the thirty-fourth year of his reign (circa 1245 BC). Many copies of this commemorative document were written for propaganda purposes. The copies were kept in the main sanctuaries and one of these, with the complete text, was found in Karnak in front of the ninth pylon of the southern propylaea.

At the time, the Hittites formed the main opposition to the Egyptians' expansionist policies. However, because their armies were of comparable strength, they reached a peaceful agreement of collaboration between the two nations which included the drawing up of a treaty establishing their respective areas of influence in the Syro-Palestinian region. Apart from the Hittite princess and other brides, Ramses II had two great wives: Isitnofret and Nefertari-Merenmut, often depicted together with the pharaoh. In accordance with tradition, the pharaoh had many children, in fact some had more than a hundred.

# The Temple of Luxor

On the preceding pages is a view of a part of the Temple of Luxor, between the entrance and Amenophis III's colonnade. The widest part of the Nile can be seen in the background.

The architectural history of the Temple of Luxor began with the reign of Amenophis III and ended with Ramses II's additions. Ramses II's entrance pylon is preceded by an obelisk over 25m tall. The second obelisk of the pair was taken to Paris in 1836 and now stands in Place de la Concorde. Colossi of Ramses II, – two cult objects seated (15.60m tall) and four standing – were all positioned in front of the pylon. The peristyle court extends behind the pylon where colossi of the pharaoh (originally Amenophis III, then replaced by Ramses II) were placed between the columns on the southern side. Ramses II had a chapel constructed to honour the Theban Triad to the right of the entrance, with three cellae behind the pylon bordered by a fine colonnade probably built at some point during the Middle Kingdom. The mosque dedicated to Abu l-Haggag, husband of the virgin and Christian martyr, Dalcina, stands on the former site of a church on the opposite side of the court. This Islamic building can be seen on the opposite page. Behind the court, Amenophis III's imposing, detached colonnade heralds the entrance to the temple itself. It is enclosed by two walls on which Tutankhamen and Haremhab had an entire procession from Karnak carved with great realism and elegance. The rear of the temple was solely the work of Amenophis III. It consists of a peristyle court leading into a hypostyle hall which enters, through two vestibules, the central cella where Amun's processional barque was kept. This cella is flanked by smaller rooms including the Hall of Divine Descent where the legend of the pharaoh's divine origin is depicted. The small rooms to either side of the first vestibule were dedicated to the goddess Mut and the god Khons. The chapel for the effigy of the god was at the rear. All the temple's external walls, engraved with various battle scenes, were decorated by Ramses II.

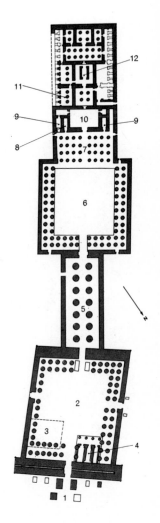

1 Obelisk, Statue and Pylon of Ramses I
2 Ramses II's Court
3 Mosque of Abu l-Haggag
4 Chapel of the Theban Triad
5 Amenophis III Colonnade
6 Amenophis III Court
7 Hypostyle Hall
8 Chapel dedicated to Mut
9 Chapel dedicated to Khons
10 Chapel of the Roman Legion
11 Hall of Divine Descent
12 Sanctuary for the Barque of Amun

The Temple of Luxor is the southern sanctuary of the god Amun, here taking on the ithyphallic form of Min. Once a year during the festival of Opet, the god left his Karnak dwelling-place to visit his hypostasis in Luxor. A great procession accompanied the god's barque down the long avenue of human-headed sphinxes connecting the two sanctuaries – in the photograph we can see the final part near the pylon of the Temple of Luxor – pausing at four points. The homes of the people were built on either side of the avenue, on the other side of a low wall. These included villas and palaces but also labourers' houses. The avenue as we see it today was created by Nectanebo I and was recently excavated underneath the Roman city which later covered the entire area. By the pylon, originally preceded by six colossi of Ramses II and two pink granite obelisks, are two statues of the pharaoh, an obelisk and other sculptures. Its towers, 24m tall, cover an area 65m wide marked by four apertures used to insert the banner-poles.

*Below: Ramses II head from a colossus in front of the temple pylon. Opposite: reliefs and inscriptions commemorating the battle of Kadesh, in which Ramses II fought against the Hittites, can be seen engraved on the pylon. On the western tower of the pylon, the pharaoh had himself depicted receiving his vanguard's reports, with an illustration of the chaos in the Egyptian camp when it was overcome by its enemies. The battle during which the king repelled the attack and claimed final victory is depicted on the eastern tower.*

*Statues of Amenophis III, later appropriated by Ramses II located between the columns of the first court where every available space was filled with effigies. A cryptographic inscription can be seen on the architrave. Next to the pharaoh are much smaller statues of Queen Nefertari, Ramses II's wife, or Bintanat, his daughter. Eleven of the statues in the southern part of the courtyard are made of red granite, and another much smaller one in grey granite. There is also a double row of seventy-four columns with closed papyrus-shaped capitals.*

In the south-west corner of the first court is an illustration of the procession of large bulls. They are adorned with flowers for sacrifice and are being led to the temple by a long procession of priests (below, a detail). Ramses II's seventeen children, who led the procession during the inauguration of the great pylon of Luxor (bottom), precede them. The pylon is again represented in this series of reliefs (not visible in the photograph), described in detail with its banners, obelisks and statues.

Shown on these pages is the chapel dedicated to the Theban Triad in the first court of the Temple of Luxor, behind the pylon's southern tower. This chapel was probably built by Ramses II who used older building material, including the fine monolithic columns. It was one of the stopping points for the sacred barque during the procession which transferred it between Karnak and Luxor. The entire layout of the first court, which Ramses II added to the front of Amenophis III's building, conforms to a peculiarity of Egyptian architecture: all the finest examples of building (like art, literature and worship) had supposedly been designed in the distant past by the gods themselves, so the way to improve them was not so much to create new forms but to extend the existing buildings, making them even grander. This explains the typology of this particular architecture, in which the buildings were developed through continous additions. It is also the origin of their stylistic uniformity throughout the centuries.

*Below: a view of Amenophis III's colonnades, elegantly gracing the
Temple of Luxor. The photograph shows both the entrance
colonnade and the colonnade surrounding the courtyard in two
rows, covering an area of 52 by 20m. Opposite: a foreshortened
internal view of the rear of the chapel dedicated to the Theban Triad.
The colonnade was bordered on the east and west by two large walls
on which Tutankhamen and Haremhab had inscribed scenes of the
procession of the sacred barque. To start with, on the western wall,
the barques of the Theban gods and that of the pharaoh are shown in*

*their sanctuaries. Then, after the statutory offerings, they are shown
being carried outside the temple on the priests' shoulders, floated on
the water and then towed by barges in full sail, with the oarsmen in
position, while music, dance and the crowd of followers accompany
them on the river banks. On arriving in Luxor, they are greeted
with honours and sacrifices. The return to Karnak is depicted on the
eastern wall. The reliefs were extemely realistic, once again showing
traces of El Amârna art in its later period. In the foreground one can
see the ruins of Byzantine churches.*

*Below: the corridor, surrounding the sanctuary for the sacred barque, built by Alexander of Macedonia in place of a former hypostyle chamber. The arched door dates from the Coptic period when Christianity was introduced into the temple. Opposite: the columns surrounding and supporting the ceiling of the room dedicated to the sovereign's divine descent. The legend of Amun, in the form Pharaoh Tuthmosis IV, being united with Queen Mutemuia, who gave birth to Amenophis III is actually depicted.*

# Index